Graham

By George Forbes

D0488470

Lang**Syne**
PUBLISHING
WRITING *to* REMEMBER

Lang**Syne**

PUBLISHING

WRITING *to* REMEMBER

79 Main Street, Newtongrange,
Midlothian EH22 4NA
Tel: 0131 344 0414   Fax: 0845 075 6085
E-mail: info@lang-syne.co.uk
www.langsyneshop.co.uk

Design by Dorothy Meikle
Printed by Ricoh Print Scotland
© Lang Syne Publishers Ltd 2013

ISBN 978-1-85217-091-2

Graham

SEPT NAMES INCLUDE:
Allardice
Bontein
Bontine
Bunten
Graeme
MacGilvernock
Monteith
Doig

Graham

MOTTO:
Ne oublie
(Do Not Forget).

CREST:
A Falcon Wings Displayed Proper
with Gold Beak and Talons Preying
on a Silver Stork with Red Claws.

TERRITORY:
the Trossachs, Perthshire,
Dundee, Montrose.

Chapter one:

The origins of the clan system

by Rennie McOwan

The original Scottish clans of the Highlands and the great families of the Lowlands and Borders were gatherings of families, relatives, allies and neighbours for mutual protection against rivals or invaders.

Scotland experienced invasion from the Vikings, the Romans and English armies from the south. The Norman invasion of what is now England also had an influence on land-holding in Scotland. Some of these invaders stayed on and in time became 'Scottish'.

The word clan derives from the Gaelic language term 'clann', meaning children, and it was first used many centuries ago as communities were formed around tribal lands in glens and mountain fastnesses.

The format of clans changed over the centuries, but at its best the chief and his family held the land on behalf of all, like trustees, and the ordinary clansmen and women believed they had a blood relationship with the founder of their clan.

There were two way duties and obligations. An inadequate chief could be deposed and replaced by someone of greater ability.

Clan people had an immense pride in race. Their relationship with the chief was like adult children to a father and they had a real dignity.

The concept of clanship is very old and a more feudal notion of authority gradually crept in.

Pictland, for instance, was divided into seven principalities ruled by feudal leaders who were the strongest and most charismatic leaders of their particular groups.

By the sixth century the 'British' kingdoms of Strathclyde, Lothian and Celtic Dalriada (Argyll) had emerged and Scotland, as one nation, began to take shape in the time of King Kenneth MacAlpin.

Some chiefs claimed descent from

ancient kings which may not have been accurate in every case.

By the twelfth and thirteenth centuries the clans and families were more strongly brought under the central control of Scottish monarchs.

Lands were awarded and administered more and more under royal favour, yet the power of the area clan chiefs was still very great.

The long wars to ensure Scotland's independence against the expansionist ideas of English monarchs extended the influence of some clans and reduced the lands of others.

Those who supported Scotland's greatest king, Robert the Bruce, were awarded the territories of the families who had opposed his claim to the Scottish throne.

In the Scottish Borders country – the notorious Debatable Lands – the great families built up a ferocious reputation for providing warlike men accustomed to raiding into England and occasionally fighting one another.

Chiefs had the power to dispense justice and to confiscate lands and clan warfare produced a society where martial virtues – courage, hardiness, tenacity – were greatly admired.

Gradually the relationship between the clans and the Crown became strained as Scottish monarchs became more orientated to life in the Lowlands and, on occasion, towards England.

The Highland clans spoke a different language, Gaelic, whereas the language of Lowland Scotland and the court was Scots and in more modern times, English.

Highlanders dressed differently, had different customs, and their wild mountain land sometimes seemed almost foreign to people living in the Lowlands.

It must be emphasised that Gaelic culture was very rich and story-telling, poetry, piping, the clarsach (harp) and other music all flourished and were greatly respected.

Highland culture was different from other parts of Scotland but it was not inferior or less sophisticated.

Central Government, whether in London or Edinburgh, sometimes saw the Gaelic clans as

"The spirit of the clan means much to thousands of people"

a challenge to their authority and some sent
expeditions into the Highlands and west to crush
the power of the Lords of the Isles.

Nevertheless, when the eighteenth century
Jacobite Risings came along the cause of the
Stuarts was mainly supported by Highland clans.

The word Jacobite comes from the Latin
for James – Jacobus. The Jacobites wanted to
restore the exiled Stuarts to the throne of Britain.

The monarchies of Scotland and England
became one in 1603 when King James VI of
Scotland (1st of England) gained the English
throne after Queen Elizabeth died.

The Union of Parliaments of Scotland and
England, the Treaty of Union, took place in 1707.

Some Highland clans, of course, and
Lowland families opposed the Jacobites and
supported the incoming Hanoverians.

After the Jacobite cause finally went down
at Culloden in 1746 a kind of ethnic cleansing took
place. The power of the chiefs was curtailed.
Tartan and the pipes were banned in law.

Many emigrated, some because they

wanted to, some because they were evicted by force. In addition, many Highlanders left for the cities of the south to seek work.

Many of the clan lands became home to sheep and deer shooting estates.

But the warlike traditions of the clans and the great Lowland and Border families lived on, with their descendants fighting bravely for freedom in two world wars.

Remember the men from whence you came, says the Gaelic proverb, and to that could be added the role of many heroic women.

The spirit of the clan, of having roots, whether Highland or Lowland, means much to thousands of people.

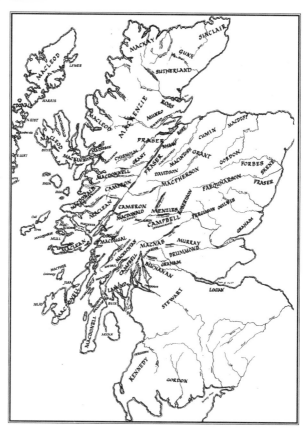

A map of the clans' homelands

Chapter two:

True patriots

The name Graham rings like a clarion trumpet call down through the colourful pageant of Scottish history.

Their courageous allegiance to the royal house of Scotland through thick and thin gave them a reputation for loyalty that has stood the test of time (despite the fact that one of them, Sir Robert Graham, slew James I at the Blackfriars Royal Lodge in Perth in 1437 in the belief that a regal dictatorship was being imposed).

One colourful tradition relates how Greme was a mighty Caledonian warrior who broke the Antonine Wall and helped drive the Romans out of Scotland, the breach in the defences ever after being known as Graeme's Dyke.

But it is much more likely that the family actually came over with William the Conqueror in the eleventh century and is Anglo-Norman in origin. A Manor of Gregham or Greyhome is recorded in the Conqueror's Domesday Book.

When King David I came to Scotland to claim his throne, a Graham was among the knights who accompanied him; while Sir William de Graham was present at the building of the Abbey of Holyrood and witnessed its foundation charter.

The Grahams fought staunchly alongside both Wallace and Bruce during the long struggle for Scottish independence and were suitably rewarded, the first lands the family acquired being around Dalkeith in Midlothian.

The Grahams' acceptance in Celtic Scotland was assured when they married into the princely family of Strathearn; and from Malise of Strathearn they acquired the lands around Auchterarder that were to become their principal seat.

Sir John de Graham was a legendary warrior among Wallace's followers and was known as 'Graham with the bright sword'. He fell, fighting to the last, at the battle of Falkirk in

1298 and his gravestone and effigy can still be found in the local kirkyard near the battle site.

The family's lands and power gradually grew and they acquired an estate at Mugdock, north of Glasgow, where they built an imposing castle in 1370.

Patrick Graham of Kincardine was created a peer in 1451 with the title of Lord Graham; and two generations later they were created Earls of Montrose.

The first Earl fell at the bloodsoaked massacre of Flodden in 1513: but by means of purchase, inheritance and inter-marriage, the Graham lands had become, by the late seventeenth century, among the richest in Scotland.

Chapter three:

The mighty Marquis

The most famous clansman was undoubtedly the fifth Earl and first Marquis of Montrose, James Graham.

When the General Assembly met in St. Mungo's Cathedral in 1638 to depose the Scottish bishops, Montrose, as an elder of the church, was one of its members; and he denounced King Charles I for his arrogant over-stepping of the royal prerogative by forcing a Book of Common Prayer upon and generally anglicising the northern Presbyterians.

Up to that point Montrose, aged 26, had been an average aristocrat of his time: but he now signed the National Covenant (an anti-Royalist petition defending the Church of Scotland and enforcing its independence) and organised a rebel army, leading troops against the Earl of Huntly and beating royalist forces at the Brig o' Dee.

But Montrose was gradually becoming

The First Marquis of Montrose

*James Graham, the fifth Earl and first
Marquis of Montrose*

disillusioned with the civil turmoil engendered by
the Covenant. While negotiating with Charles, to
whom he still retained an emotional loyalty,
he was busy putting forward solutions in
Covenanting councils: but gradually his royalist
sympathies came to the fore, especially when it
was revealed that his arch enemy and champion of
the Kirk, Archibald Campbell, Earl of Argyll, was
being touted as a future dictator.

Montrose accused Campbell of treason
thus upsetting his former Covenanting colleagues.
He refused to support the Scottish Parliament's
union with the English Roundheads, effectively
set up by the Solemn League and Covenant of
1643, and was imprisoned for five months in
Edinburgh Castle.

Although still courted to take command
of the Covenanting forces, he had made his mind
up and turned down such blandishments. From
now on he was to be a King's man or nothing.

At the age of 32, he joined Charles at
Oxford and convinced him of his loyalty,
receiving a commission as lieutenant general in

Scotland and embarking on the most exciting period of his life.

In August, 1644, he was in the Highlands, raising his army from among a wild rabble who recognised the opportunity of striking a blow against the fiefdom of the wealthy Campbells.

His forces were also boosted by an Ulster contingent led by the fierce warrior Alasdair MacColla, a MacDonald with great strength and military expertise who had a bitter hatred of the Clan Campbell. He commanded 2,000 men, composed of Catholic veterans of Irish wars and Highland refugees. Their specialty was the notorious Highland Charge which involved firing a single volley from their muskets then charging the enemy with wooden shields and flashing broadswords, a ferocious, screaming mass of clansmen with their blood up. This was a decisive tactic which usually led to the Covenanters taking to their heels, many of them being cut down as they fled the wild onslaught.

Capturing Perth after a furious clash beneath its walls when the Royalist force decimated an army three times its size, Montrose, thus encouraged, recklessly determined to win Scotland for Charles and, at the same time, divert enemy troops from his beleaguered sovereign down south.

Montrose marched to Aberdeen which was quickly taken: but the bold Marquis for once had a moral lapse, allowing his troops to ransack the city in an orgy of rape and pillage (more than a hundred peaceful citizens were brutally murdered).

The Royalist army then headed through Strathbogie to Speyside and turned south through Badenoch to Atholl.

Argyll was now in hot pursuit and the Royalists destroyed anything that might sustain their enemies while the Covenanters cruelly punished anyone remotely suspected of helping the rebels.

Winter bogged down the pursuit and Alasdair suggested a daring march through the mountains to fall on the Argyll heartlands. This was done, bringing carnage to Inveraray at Christmas and Argyll, racing to rescue his homelands, ended up fleeing down Loch Fyne in a galley, leaving his clansmen to their bloody fate.

The jubilant Royalists then withdrew to the north, crossing into Lochaber and marching up the Great Glen where they were caught in a pincer movement between the Earl of Seaforth marching down from Inverness and fresh troops rallied by Argyll coming up from Inverlochy.

But Montrose and Alasdair were not so easily put down and they turned into the hills at the south end of Loch Ness where they doubled back behind the snowy mountains and caught Argyll's army by surprise in the rear. More than 1,500 Campbell clansmen were slaughtered and the bards of Keppoch celebrated the event for decades afterwards.

Montrose and his army went on to a succession of stunning victories at Auldearn, Alford and Kilsyth.

In a brilliant year he had cleared much of Scotland of the King's enemies and if the Royalist forces south of the border had been even remotely as competent and ruthless then Charles would not have lost his head and the course of British history would have been changed.

But already national events were working against Montrose. He was unable to recruit the support of the nobility and had antagonised various factions. Meanwhile, Alasdair left his side to continue his own personal vendetta against the Campbells of Argyll; and a lack of an intelligence arm to Montrose's forces meant that he consistently underestimated his opponents and was in the dark with regards to their actions. At Philiphaugh, outside Selkirk, this was to prove calamitous on 13th September, 1645.

Here Montrose finally came up against a worthy opponent – David Leslie, the best of the Covenanting generals, brilliant and brutal, who was marching north to deal with the upstart at the head of a force of 6,000 men, more than 5,000 of whom were cavalry.

The Royalists moved up the Tweed in the vain hope of raising the Border clans and camped on a strong position in front of a hill surrounded by streams.

At daybreak a dense autumn mist lay over the camp and the sentries could not see the approach of Leslie's horsemen who had forded the Ettrick during the night, although pickets had vaguely warned of an enemy force in the area.

As the sun broke through the greyness, the Covenanter troopers were ready to charge while the Royalists were still finishing breakfast. Montrose was billeted in a lodging at Selkirk when the alarm was raised; he jumped on a horse and galloped to his camp where he found his men fighting for their lives, though some of their comrades had deserted at the first charge.

Fortunately for the Royalists, they had taken the precaution of building up defensive earthworks and these proved vital in fending off attack after attack which the Covenanters, sensing victory, rained down on them.

Gradually the rebels were beaten back behind dry-stone dykes beside a farm and fought hand-to-hand until more than 400 were cut down.

Montrose rallied a hundred horsemen and led them in a mad charge which was repeated again and again: but each time the Royalists were beaten back by superior forces.

The remainder of Leslie's cavalry, on the opposite bank of the Ettrick, saw the brave but futile efforts of the Royalists, forded the river and attacked from the flank.

Six hundred Royalists had stood bravely and defiantly against a vastly superior enemy force. Only a handful survived, among them Montrose who was miraculously unhurt and prepared to die in action. But he was talked out of this by his immediate entourage, their argument being that his King would need his services in future.

He rode to Clydesdale then northwards and soon was taking refuge in the Perthshire hills, eventually fleeing abroad.

He later invaded the north of Scotland with a band of mercenaries who were ambushed and decimated, their leader eventually being betrayed in Assynt for a bag of gold.

Dressed immaculately – more like a bridegroom than a convicted criminal, according to one witness – Montrose was hanged then disembowelled at the Mercat Cross in Edinburgh, though in 1888 his remains were entombed in a splendid marble memorial in St. Giles Cathedral.

Chapter four:

Bonnie Dundee

Another famous clansman and a distant kinsman of the Marquis was John Graham of Claverhouse, known colloquially as 'Bonnie Dundee'.

He was the elder son of Royalists and claimed descent from King Robert I. While serving abroad he saved the life of the future King William of Orange in 1674; and, returning to Scotland, commanded an Independent Troop of Horse specially raised to brutally suppress open air prayer meetings held in defiance of the government, earning the nickname 'Bluidy Clavers' because of the brutality of his actions.

In the 1679 Covenanters' rebellion, he was defeated at Drumclog in Lanarkshire, then helped defend Glasgow and fought back in a victory at Bothwell Brig.

Elevated to the position of Viscount Dundee, he became a Jacobite commander in

*Clan warfare produced a society where
courage and tenacity were greatly admired*

1689, raising his standard on Dundee Law, after which he joined Lochiel's Highland Confederacy.

Over the next four months he put his army through 800 miles of rapid marching before defeating the government forces at the battle of Killiecrankie.

However, Claverhouse was shot from his horse at the moment of victory and died later that night. Without his charismatic leadership, the rebellion petered out.

Another notable clansman was the third Duke of Montrose who, as Marquis of Graham, M.P., secured the repeal of the ban on tartan brought in after the '45 Rebellion.

The story of 'the Grahams of the Hens' concerned some Stewarts of Appin who, on their way home after a campaign, stopped at the house of the Earl of Menteith to ask for food.

The Earl and his men were away hunting but the servants were busy roasting chickens for a wedding feast. The Stewarts helped themselves then went on their way.

The returning Earl was furious, gathered his clan and set off in pursuit.

When he caught up with the Stewarts, a fierce fight took place during which the Earl, many of his men and most of the Stewarts were killed or mortally wounded.

The name 'Grahams of the Hens' stuck from that day on, as some Highland onlookers thought it a terrible waste of life over a few roast chickens. But pride had been at stake and that was something no Graham could ever overlook.

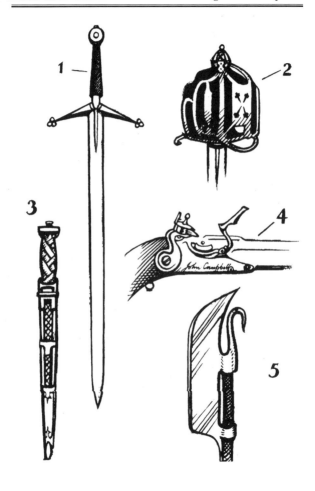

Highland weapons

1)   The claymore or two-handed sword
     (fifteenth or early sixteenth century)

2)   Basket hilt of broadsword
     made in Stirling, 1716

3)   Highland dirk
     (eighteenth century)

4)   Steel pistol *(detail)* made in Doune

5)   Head of Lochaber Axe as carried
     in the '45 and earlier